FOR THE LOST CATHEDRAL

FOR THE
LOST CATHEDRAL

❧ POEMS ❧

BRUCE BOND

LOUISIANA STATE UNIVERSITY PRESS | BATON ROUGE

Published with the assistance of the Sea Cliff Fund

Published by Louisiana State University Press
Copyright © 2015 by Bruce Bond
All rights reserved
Manufactured in the United States of America
LSU Press Paperback Original
First printing

Designer: Laura Roubique Gleason
Typeface: Whitman
Printer and binder: Lightning Source

Library of Congress Cataloging-in-Publication Data
Bond, Bruce, 1954–
  [Poems. Selections]
  For the lost cathedral : poems / Bruce Bond.
    pages ; cm
  ISBN 978-0-8071-5962-0 (pbk. : alk. paper) — ISBN 978-0-8071-5963-7 (pdf)
— ISBN 978-9807159647 (epub) — ISBN 978-0-8071-5965-1 (mobi)
  I. Title.
  PS3552.O5943A6 2015
  811'.54—dc23

                                                    2014026206

The paper in this book meets the guidelines for permanence and durability
of the Committee on Production Guidelines for Book Longevity of the
Council on Library Resources. ⊚

When it came night, the white waves paced to and fro in the moonlight, and the wind brought the sound of the great sea's voice to the men on the shore, and they felt that they could then be interpreters.

—STEPHEN CRANE, "The Open Boat"

CONTENTS

❧ III ❦

❧ IV ❦

ACKNOWLEDGMENTS

I would like to thank the editors of the following journals in which versions of these poems first appeared: *Battistrada Arts Review:* "For the Lost Cathedral" (section 7); *Blackbird:* "For the Lost Cathedral" (sections 6, 9, and 11); *Conte:* "Via Negativa"; *Crab Orchard Review:* "Sleeper"; *The Georgia Review:* "Proud Flesh"; *Great River Review:* "Air"; *Harvard Review:* "The Bone Church of Sedlic"; *The Hopkins Review:* "Gargoyle"; *Image:* "Advent," "Homage to a Philosopher of History as a Small Child," "Hymn," "Monotheism," and "The Raising of the Bells"; *The Iowa Review:* "Blink"; *The Journal:* "The Dead Zoo" and "Mirror"; *The Mayo Review:* "For the Lost Cathedral" (sections 4 and 8); *The Missouri Review:* "The Last Great Flood"; *Pleiades:* "The Gate"; *Quadrant: Journal of the C. G. Jung Foundation for Analytical Psychology:* "Canaan"; *Raritan:* "Idolatry" and "The Winds"; *Saint Katherine's Review:* "Homage to William Blake"; *The Saint Petersburg Review:* "Threnody"; *The Seattle Review:* "The Unspeakable"; *The Sewanee Review:* "Lebensraum" and "Tallow"; *Shade:* "For the Lost Cathedra" (sections 1–3, 5, and 10); *The Southern Review:* "Trinity"; *32 Poems:* "The Missing Link"; *TriQuarterly:* "Harvest"; *Virginia Quarterly Review:* "The Water Clock"; *Zone 3:* "The Desert Fathers" and "Purity."

"The Last Great Flood" appeared also in *Quarterly Review of Literature Poetry Series: 50th Anniversary Anthology.* In addition, the poem "Sand" was featured by *Verse Daily.* "The Winds," "Masters of the Plein Air," "Harvest," "The Unspeakable," and sections 3 and 5 of "For the Lost Cathedral" were republished in *Battistrada Arts Review;* "Advent" was republished in the *Poetry Calendar 2013* (Belgium, Alhambra Press), and the poem "Threnody" won the Saint Petersburg Review Poetry Prize.

❧ | ❧

THE GATE

When first I came into the world,
I wept at the sting of light
and steel that cut me as I gasped.

The black rain kindled a quiet
fire in the window, and I listened
to a distance that had no language.

That was the 50s, when Asia
slept beneath a drizzle of ash
that had been falling since the war.

When I first learned of heaven,
it was something we lost, or was
loss simply the word we gave it.

When I heard my nation's stories,
they were the words of a father
who gave me words. I was what I feared.

If there is a pearl gate up there,
I see it as a guillotine
that chooses its friends carefully.

The eye of the needle, the narrow
passage, they would straighten us.
The sound of rain would make us open.

ADVENT

On an island in the disputed region
of the Yellow Sea, blooms of smoke
from the shelling of the garrison
weave into one bloom, one force of nature
so thick, they say, you cannot see your hands.
The planet, we know, tilts on its axis
like a man contemplating a problem,
spun toward the horizon of another
year, always forward, across a winter
where we celebrate an advent so long
past it could have been most any season.
Islanders will tell you, the farther back
you go the more it dims into a future,
the one we carry as a grudge or gift
to lay at the threshold of a child's bed.
Nights when the cold draws its curtain
on our homes, we turn to the windows
of TVs and stare, alone with the war
and its commercials, the firestorm
that breaks a motherland in two like bread.
We too break, each year a little more
divided at heart as we cough by the fire,
still and sleepy as cows in the crèche,
thinking it is one thing for a king
to kneel, another for him to seek advice.
The modern kings do not wander far
into the desert but tend to sit and watch
the monitors fill up with falling lights.
Facts are hard, like the man who buries
his hatchet in the turkey he shares
with a neighbor, with talk that turns bitter
as it grows more national in scope.
Say I am the offspring of the thought
I just had, flesh of its flesh, and so

different, in some measure culpable, free,
as anything alive. A child is born,
crowned in blood, and we lighten up.
Sure, we see it every day, and yet
this day, tradition says, is unlike any,
which is true. It has never happened,
and never will again, over and over
the will to be reborn, to gasp and cry
forgiveness, that is, like birth, difficult,
scared, insurgent, brave with the stranger,
the winter child, that blossoms through the wound.

SLEEPER

As a boy, I took a night train over the border,
above acres of tenements and town squares

locked in the black box of winter. *Go home,*
said the quiet streets, just beyond the scrawl

of graffiti and electric wire that held us, bound
for West Berlin. Everywhere the unspoken

contract with a past no boy could understand,
let alone me, there, behind the passenger window,

my bleached face gone dim as the dark fell through.
Block after block the dull terror of cities

like warehouse districts alive with citizens—
they must be out there somewhere—though who was I to say.

Late came early in the heart of the regime,
or so I imagined as I slept, best I could,

the train shuddering like a waterfall around me.
In time the noise whitened to an emptiness

that drowned the inner ear, a veil over the voices,
which in turn veiled the silence of the season.

There, in my sleep, I could not sleep, and so stepped
into the city, looking for a lamp in the glaze

of some chained window, a curtain to rustle,
a code to crack. Which is when I caught my own eye

in the glass, collar turned against the wind,
and asked, who am I to trust the person that I see.

December made the stars harder, their secrecy
more ruthless. What I would not give to sleep

a deeper sleep, and so I lay in the snow,
weary as an hourglass, feeling less and less,

as all the while a locomotive in the distance
plunged farther to the north, to the chamber of engines

where a boxcar from Warsaw went still, latched in horror,
and the smell of chimneys drifted through the door.

CROSS OF NAILS

The morning after the blitzkrieg that toppled the vaults
of Saint Michael's Cathedral and set the rest on fire,

a stonemason found among the embers one roof
beam laid across another, a kind of crucifix

created by the forces of accident and violence
and then by grace of eyes that saw in them an order.

A puzzler of rubble and its hidden logic,
he chiseled the words *Father, forgive,* then lashed and raised

the crux into a monument, an abstract man,
beneath the gutted tower left unrepaired for good.

Forgiveness forgets nothing—any cross will tell you—
but calls as witness a common father to ask of us

what we then would ask of him. *Forgive them, Father,*
says the reddened letters in the large black book

that, some claim, is God talking to God, or a man
to men, or both at once. Oh, it gets confusing,

the dust that falls for weeks over the bombed cathedral
as the search party lays its dead in the street.

Coventry, Dresden, Berlin, they know a thing or two
about confusion, the grief that makes a home a stranger,

a stranger a home in ruins you think you understand.
You do and do not, and the things that go unsaid

are tender sometimes as wounds are and certain mothers,
certain gathering storms that call their children in.

As roofs go, so go their nails, and the oldest ones
were so long and fierce, the men of Saint Michael's

torched three into the mastlike symbol of their faith,
the vertical axis with its dagger toward the earth.

And they gave it away, shipped it across the channel.
Walk the ruins of the Keiser Wilhelm Church,

and you see there the heavy iron nails raised up
like an anchor drawn to heaven's invisible hull.

Call it confession or kindness, it is, and no less sharp
than all that make forgiveness possible and hard.

It is specific, as givers and receivers are.
And yes, it would raise us up in turn. And yes,

it is still a nail and so longs to be struck,
immersed, remembered. Call it the drizzle of soot,

the inconsolable cry, the widows of England
facedown in their pillows. Call it what you will,

this stake in the nation, the heart, the corpus mundi,
this gift that would be yours. The moment that you give it.

MONOTHEISM

As he raises my bookshelf, empty now,
and therefore heavy with what I do not know,
my friend the carpenter speaks so kindly

of all the dark acolytes of one god
who walk the streets of ground zero in fear,
beneath the shadows and mistrust that pour

down the highest places like waterfalls
of dust. But those of no god or many,
he adds, well, they are another matter.

Then a nail goes in, and I am standing
before the space where Ovid will one day stand
by a Bible, beside, in turn, the lovers

of doubt who watched God vanish through a hole
and followed deep into the echo, knowing
less, step by step. Each waits for a reader,

the way a laurel tree waits for one to listen,
to sit beside the river and so drink
the words of the dead into those we speak.

Narcissus enters the mirror like a plane,
and we anticipate some flower or other
to take his place, to rise alone, and scatter.

I like to think of Ovid's son as sweetened
by his father's voice, still as a tree
that long ago was just a tree. Imagine.

My friend's hands make of wood something
strong with beauty, and I see these shelves
as one world, beloved. One maker, he would say,

and the words go out to the rain, the root,
the author's boy beneath the tiny freedoms
of the leaves, one child among the many,

whose will to choose is the god in each.

VIA NEGATIVA

for Paul Tillich

Our godless god, our one
no one, our all things small,
our no thing in particular,
our wind in the belfry
bronzed with fading praise,
remember, when my candles
offered up their shadows,
you were no god to me,
and so I turned instead
to the act of turning,
the prayer I offered up
as I looked down, each word
floating through my back.
And in my vigil, I saw
a bug on the carpet,
a sapphire of a creature,
as it scuttled, stopped, chose,
in faith, a new direction.
Spirit is cheap, I thought.
No. Cheaper. It's free.
Its legs move the clockwork
in the great world machine
of small decisions, spiriting
from here to there, to nowhere
in the narrative scripture.
Back then I feared all
the wrong things and touched
the blue beneath the kettle.
The bigger I got, the tougher
the freedoms, the bluer the flame.
If only the future were
some beneficent tyrant.

How unbearably clear.
Instead I woke my father
to sweep the phantom insects
from my bed. It's nothing,
he said. And with that,
I pulled my blanket, sealed
the dark in something darker.
Nothing, nothing echoed.
It still does. I have no father,
no earth but this. The path
into sleep is the same
long passage into morning.
I choose therefore I am
chosen, spoken. I speak.
Therefore I leave this ghost,
my voice's voice, behind.

PURITY

I am God.
　　—ALEXANDER SCRIABIN

In Moscow once, you could close your eyes
and see music sweep the German army
into the Black Sea, into valleys with all

their poverty and smoke, the lettuce fields
reduced to char, to trophies, blue steel,
the spire of a helmet with no one in it.

Somewhere a composer trimmed his beard,
in his head a last song he never knew
was last, only that it would celebrate

The Great War, earth purged in a deluge
of flies. But then, what does a song know.
The news embedded in the music remains

just that, buried in a mound of flowers.
The composer snipped his moustache and mused,
his hair so thick he could not see the boil

break. A war cuts so many blossoms
to lie among, so many invocations,
clouds of dust fading like an anthem.

If the man there deepened the infection,
was it one more sign among many.
Did he still read the world as a book

he authored, where the cathedrals welled
with tunes, prayers to carry all our sins
into some dark booth, to leave this life

spotless, without the pride that spits on things
to make them shine. In Budapest once,
people emerged from their homes to listen,

their skies gone clear at last, as somewhere high
on the banks of the Danube a church tolled
for those whose names laid down inside the living.

The sound of bells shuddered in the mirror,
in the mourners who came and went like music.
And when the music stopped, they shuddered still.

MIRROR

for Hannah Arendt

The day the jet entered the building's mirror
to nail its version of heaven to the sky,
the smoke that lingered asked, is this it,

not paradise, but some vision of it
reaching back to pull us through the fire.
Make yourself useful, my father told me,

and I loved him with a love that was
no project. It seemed odd, how the imperfect
end all too perfectly in what they fear

no more. *Sit still,* my mother told me,
and sunlight bled through the great rose window.
It scared me, the thought of salvation.

What is it to nail your own convictions
to a church door, if only to look back
at this thing you call your life. But it is not life.

Does it come as some relief, to see
your name dissipate the way rain must,
and will, or our mothers with their song.

Terror's pilots never learned to land.
Did they too look back at their lives
as they approached them in the mirror.

The world's end reflects us all, naturally,
we who plan our retirements with an eye
to small comforts, debts, a minimum of stairs.

I believed early on death was invented
to press questions made more rewarding
without answers. I ask my work daily,

What, in the end, is the use of use?
When I look at the dead still photo
of my father, I do not see him. Not yet.

Begin again, says the brittle winter
dawn. Which for the moment is enough.
Day's honey pouring through the glass.

HARVEST

Must it be the spot upon the x-ray
that becomes our autumn cloud, our hole
to view the contents of our lives, to pray
into perhaps with the greed of the fragile
at heart. Must it be the broken will
that bends our knees to speak with the unknown.
Why the sickbed as our first cathedral,
or the ailing father our wafer, our wine.
Why must the well of the oracle
call back from its throat inside the earth
to make us into strangers as we kneel.
Somewhere beyond the mirror of our death,
we were light once, thrown open, ever near
to what, we could not say, blind with rain
that broke so fast against the back of summer,
who thought to praise its fury as we ran.

THE LAST GREAT FLOOD

Lock Haven, Pennsylvania

We live on the floodplain,
where waterfowl are plentiful
and news is mostly minor:
two deaths, a marriage.
People here know disaster
comes every twenty-some years
down the old route of logs
and immigrants. It watermarks
the diner walls, chalked high
as a boast, hangs in photographs
of ripped silos, power wires
where they broke and sputtered,
flailing into the wet street.
Not to mention the unmooring
of dumpsters and cars, Christ
Church humbled to a single story,
or the crippled spillway
of the courthouse bridge,
how the water rose to skim
and crack it, then slowly drown
the thing entire. And all along
the forest highway, perched high
above the stench and tumble
of the mist: the sudden cliffs
that shuddered and slipped,
gone the way of their deep
foundation. Unlikely still,
which is how we bear it,
own it even, why we stare
beside the blackened banks
as if to salvage some stray
doll or pair of glasses,

some swollen book. It pulls us
in, the flotilla of obscurities,
how the graves washed
open upstream, the cow
that caught the radio tower
and would not tear away.
Slow to forget, slower still
to fathom, as if each version
of the deluge held something back,
a trace inside the petulant
cloud and thunder, a bloom
of silt to ghost the broken
dragnets of the trees.
Like any story we tell to death,
ours had a little future in it.
Leave it to the bowed heads
of idleness and prayer
what grand design or indifference
surged that day, what darkened
the erasure that was our street.
Leave it to some deferred
explanation, some covenant
as sure as the flood itself.
Leave it behind if you can:
the pools of sludge that mortified
beneath the blue absolution
of the sun. Our piles of trash
rose tall as houses then. Still
it testifies to the beauty here,
to the long braid of parenthood
and poverty that make it hard
to leave. For the river carries little
now in the way of logs and profit.
Even as the airplane factory

dragged its bad steel to Jersey
for scrap, and the trains resumed,
passing through without a whistle,
we stayed on by the stream
of burials and marriage, faith
and the river that is its cure.

❧ II ❧

THRENODY

After Penderecki

In an alley where the world ends,
I have hung a door. It opens
to those who have no other
home, who walk as strangers
to these streets. I see them
always, and they are strangers still.
I hear in them a threnody
that is a field of all the notes
at once, even those that fall
between the ones we know,
joined the way that flames join
the walls of smoke and molten glass.
The architecture of memory
burns a thousand different ways,
its skin drawn back, a thousand
different silences behind it.
There are stories our forgetting
makes safe enough for grief,
embers stirred the way we stir
a tin of soup, or spare change.
A record spins on its needle.
The pages that trouble me most
crumple in the heart's furnace,
in the iron that gives off heat
years after the ash resolves.
My furnace has a latch, a door,
where a hand comes and goes,
its arm far away somewhere.
It has a hinge that sings across
the threshold, a mouth that gapes
as it listens, as it disbelieves

the news buried inside the music,
at least until the music ends
and history is a heart that opens
itself, alive, and walks right through.

THE BONE CHURCH OF SEDLIC

The door to heaven is a plot of land
in the mist and doldrums of the plains,

where long ago an abbot sprinkled a fist
of dirt from Golgotha and so brought his god

a little closer, holding open the grave
as the plague swept the souls of Europe in.

Those were days the cries of boarded windows
spread like rumor, and though the faithful

put the lion's share of trust in Jesus,
there were those who turned to a sacrament

of things: the monstrance, the cross, dirt
a martyr's blood made priceless. The word too,

one half spirit, the other flesh, offered
gospel to the sick who could not sleep.

Any wonder they dreamt of the fields
of Sedlic. The door to heaven is small,

uncertainty enormous, and so they came,
the multitudes, bones exhumed to make room

for the new who kept arriving in carts,
the still warm, still-remembered lives.

The older the skeletons, the more porous,
cleansed of the story that put them there.

And when there were bodies enough, some
sixty thousand give or take, a mass

grave in the ossuary basement, an artist
came to make of them a chapel, the angels

of dismantled parts without shame
or anguish draped about the crucifix.

He even hung a chandelier with a skull
in each wing crowned in candlelight,

so the shadows cast shadows against the altar.
A Christ could get lost in the wilderness

of little heads, so plentiful they became
more than human, less than animal.

The soul tears from its scaffold like a name,
until *Christ* remains the name among them,

his bones gone as these wait to die again.
What they do have is a place, the eyes

of thousands passing through as the forgotten
pass through the acre of those before them.

Here it is, the door to heaven, says the father,
who leaves his daughter on earth to look down

at her own strange feet, there in the distance.
Here it is, as if a father could be seen,

held, spoken to, as he in turn might speak
to her, his chapel, in this, his otherworld.

THE DEAD ZOO

The peaceable kingdom is a stone room
filled with corpses, a menagerie of jars,
large eels swallowing the lives that killed them.
And bones, pinned and wired, everywhere

the posturing of those who would lie down,
if not for us, for the skeletal glory
we give the bat, the monkey, the mastodon
who lifts his ivory burden to the sky.

We know, of course, his burden is illusion.
But in a corridor of dead birds, dead songs
do what dead songs do. They pull us in.
They lure us through the underworld of no one

in particular, where grief is dead grief,
where marvels are impersonal. Imagine
the human specimen, posed with his rifle,
Homo erectus, seen here on vacation.

Are we better than that, or too familiar,
our beloved exiled, embalmed in spirits
and last rites. Do we seal our final letters
in blood, sent to a place that no one visits.

If history has a heaven, a second wind,
is it this: a museum full of laughter,
a boy posed with his head in the open
casket. The jaw, the camera, the silent roar.

HOMAGE TO A PHILOSOPHER OF
HISTORY AS A SMALL CHILD

When he was only four, his mother spoke
to him in Latin and a sacrament
of Greek, the music of the dead tongues

raised up to speak for the root of all.
How proud they were, mother and son, bound
by rule and the game it made, the bread

they broke, word by word, on their way to chapel.
Amo, amare, amati. Then the page
of the giant door opened into silence.

And as he bowed his head in prayer, he asked,
*Where are you anyway, are you there
in paradise, or in me, listening to me.*

Or are you the speaker, however lost
in thought, this thought that is not mine alone.
His mother smiled, not long for this world,

though what did they know. *Laudamus te.*
And the dead rose up through the throats
in the loft. *Adoramus te.*

And the lamb on the window looked down,
knowing no god, no language, dead or alive.
Just a beast after all. For whom the music's

howl of praise might as well be mourning.
Amen, amo, amare. Say the day comes
death opens a door in silence, for which

Latin is one translation. Sheep, another.
Flocks of clouds rumble seaward and moan.
Spirit goes somewhere, thought the boy, it must.

A mother dies and the empty room looks
larger. Candles ache in the cathedral.
She becomes a story that listens to the words

she makes, that reads them to a boy
as if a story might be an explanation.
And in his sleep, as the sheep fall one

by one beneath the blade, they take no name
with them. Only a plea at best. A cry
in a tongue he has yet to understand.

LEBENSRAUM

When the ashes of last great war
settled on the ramshackle factories
and chapels of the Rhine, you could hear
a concertina walk the crooked alley

to beg beneath the window for a coin
or two, for some chime from the towers
of rooms and radios that held our nation.
What we wanted was out there, beyond the scars

ships cut across the river in the distance.
So when the man at the microphone spoke
with such force his German spat at us,
we listened, as if a thunderhead broke

our wings, not down, but open, less proud
than nailed to pride's surrogate, his face
a scaffold for the angry and the wounded.
Suns fell. Music faded. And in their place,

we lay and listened for the carriage wheel,
the bell, the hinge, the banner that chirped
as it descended, as one by one we fell
like coins, to shatter all the hearts of Europe.

GARGOYLE

Do not pity this face, the single horn
aching through the skin, these crude ears
large as hands, all meat and nerve, but born
of stone, netted in a web of scars.

Do not pity these cheeks stuffed with teeth,
eyes wide with appetite, a look so old
it wears something of the mask of birth,
choking on air, spitting out the world.

It gets old, the strut of birds in their filth,
this hat of wings, the boredom and the glory,
these days between heaven and the earth
it batters, the hiss of wind, the rain, the glare.

And yes, I think of jumping now and then.
Why not. Why curl the talons of my stare,
high above at the crawl of traffic, each man
a child beneath the great cathedral door.

If I can never enter, so much the better.
Spite them, the hags in the choir, their plate
of crumbs, the vanishings of smoke and prayer.
Spite the little creatures at the gate.

Some look to me as if I were the darling
of a lesser sin, the lance that drains
the boil, the curse that cures. Spite everything
that would feed me, heal me, take me in.

I may be small, but I can see forever.
At my feet the morning sun sets fire
to the rose. Look up and I am there
snug as a brick, a fly in the snare

of the vast design. Pity these walls,
if you must, the panic of the bells.
In the flower of things, I am the thorn.
Everything I prick begins to crown.

CANAAN

To cut is to connect, to bind
a covenant, a book, a wound,
our name the name of patriarchs

who say, *the lance will give you*
possession of the place, and who
does not dream of possession,

a home, a haunt, a shibboleth.
Without it you have no birthright
to divide. Besides, as history

tells us, the sky is murderous,
with more than one paradise
to torch us to a flock of stars.

In Canaan the air is signed in smoke.
Long ago I asked my father
if God loves His enemies,

does everybody get to heaven.
What of the lambs that go to slaughter
to bloody the doorways of the tribe.

Did I come into this world
a criminal, my tongue a sword,
to cut the sky from its horizon.

IDOLATRY

No end to the little sacraments
of the near at hand, the clock, the pen,
the watchful telephone, the many wires

of its nervous system a world wide web,
all of us bound, alone in our rooms
with one another, invisibly enormous.

If you too stare at the receiver and talk
until the face on the other line
lies buried beneath a grid of numbers,

it is no idol you see, only a passage,
an effigy inside its tablet, a night
that falls through the window as we sleep.

And yet it is tempting, as the connection
breaks, to leave you with some bad news
you have yet to hear, to look the phone

in the mouth, and continue conversation.
No idol. Just you and the thing as you
exchange your gifts, and since the telephone

draws its voice from out there somewhere,
you feel small in light of your other self
like a child before a statesman's statue.

My things give me comfort, I tell my fear
in jest, in the knowledge I will lose them.
Gods come and go, they say, but things,

they are immortal. Look at the teen idol,
not the person, but the headshot, the gloss,
the sheen that lights the pink above its bed.

It knows what it is to solar eclipse
the man who made it all possible.
And as such, it shields the curious

from certain blindness, to make visible
only the outline of the source, the crown,
a totality so like the human eye

with its black coin laid across the light.
In the desert once a tribe adorned
a gold calf who looked back through its boredom,

a cow after all, and a dead one at that,
bemused by their dance about the fire.
All that gold, why not eat the real thing.

If you had your choice, would you consume
a god, or kneel starved for power, with power,
humble as the brick that seals its palace.

The avenues of my city gleam with malls,
where kids like me go to watch, to say,
yes, I live among the others, with each

a face a mirror wears like a fine shirt.
I know a man who lost his wife to divorce
and so went out to walk the tall aisles

of his Kmart, drenched in the ordinary
radiance that was a love song gone bad.
One too many light bulbs to explain it.

Everywhere the half-distracted chirping
of a music, the air-conditioned tunes
that move along, that hope for better things.

It helped to return one broken object
for another, but more, just seeing people
who once had vanished in his happiness.

No malls in the land of radio silence,
in the anchorite kingdom of the north,
where the concentration camps are small

cities far below our satellites,
our glass-bottom boats that float in disbelief.
Not things, but the monotheism

of one thing, one image everywhere,
one statue with its monumental arm.
When the blind remove their bandages

to see, it is not the surgeon they turn to
with their tears, hands raised, bodies crushed
beneath their gratitude, but their dear

leader, the general, the iconography
they fear, they love, or both, the face that burns
in theirs this image of a soldier, his coat

a people's blue that touches the flesh that is
no flesh, only a god, the common cloth
of one man a nation weeps for as it kneels.

PROUD FLESH

Tough, the wound that heals
too quick and so conceals
its ache in a pride of scars,

a grave that swells the earth,
so when you want to talk
with your losses, you know where.

Some say it makes a body
strong, too strong perhaps,
stiff as some malignant thing.

Take the man who lost his wife
to cigarettes and a plot upstate
that had no use for words.

He turned around to double-up
his own smokes and hours at work,
beating his heart to hell, to raise

some veil over the emptiness
and in its place a tower.
The art of loss is slow because

difficult, difficult because slow.
Pity the nation that does not mourn
its drone of casualties overseas.

The graves of the last war will tell you.
Here I am, they say. Silent
row after row. Here I will never be.

III

THE WINDS

April arrives in a stupor of blossoms
and strange days, uneasy afternoons gone
dark beneath the thunderhead, the stones
of hail in their buckets waiting for heaven

to buckle and chafe, for the silence of birds
to speak, to be our breeze before the storm.
It's then you hear the wind chimes, absurd
inventions of no one's music. No weather horn

to call us in. Or down. Just these pieces
of a thing that could be all our things
here in the valley of the winds. Just pipes
where they startle and spin, where they sing

inside the drunken chapel of the air.
Not wind alone but how a metal swells
within the vesper tower, how it flares
the net that holds the shudder of the bells.

And though the winds may die, what god
kneels to tell us where. Let it be here
that we hang our chimes above the garden
threshold. Let stillness leave us everywhere.

THE UNSPEAKABLE

Call it the dawn of a native language,
a strange contagion of animal panic:
the fins that swam for the black fathoms,

their dire harbor, the flight of elephants
to higher ground, and the island cicadas,
the hordes of them buried in the nerves

of thickets, gone in their shells terribly still.
Which is how the Moken elders of these
waters knew the tidal swell was coming,

these people who owe their gods to the sea's
revisions, its rancor, its drag, how fish tumble
out of its mouth each day; these people

who have no word for *when,* no word for *want,*
only *give* and *take,* no word for *hello,*
none for *goodbye.* They live with what

they carry, what speeds their slender boats.
They too ask why: what, if anything, does
a wilderness know, there in the red gut

coiled like an ear; what blank slate breaks
in the shifting weight of the beast, thinking
nothing, we are taught, of its own demise,

how it comes, when it comes, to all fears.
Such is the gift, we say, of our word *death,*
as elsewhere under the crackle of palms,

in the onyx of the elephant's eye,
at the trumpet of its swift migration,
we meet a new order of wildness.

Our angry ancestors, say the visions
of the elders, as if it were personal,
the dead in the tall blue fanfare of their rage,

washing the world, though why here, why now.
A farther question. No word for *when,*
none for *want,* only the heaven inside

a handful of water. And a child listens
believing where once he would not, could not.
He is crossing over into the harbor

that floods his eye. No word for *hello,*
none for *goodbye,* as if both our coming
and going were acknowledged in silence,

by silence, or left to float upon the calm
of things not quite disappearing. Ask
the slowly draining spillway of the street

what it is to concede so much, to wash
the damaged shore of signs we leave behind.
Tough to forget. Tougher still to recall

all a body walks through to the past.
As if we could read into the loss
of language. Or that this loss were itself

a lens, clear as speech. There are days
the coral reef between knowledge and faith
dissolves. So says faith. So says the child.

Like a word still glistening in its ink.
A salamander drying in the sun.
There are days the magazine you read

opens as it closes, all our things
caught in the welter that knows no final
dawn, no rest, only the animate chain

of waves, the giant surge exhaling the way
a grown man exhales, too tired for words,
to snuff the floating lanterns of the bay.

HOMAGE TO WILLIAM BLAKE

What immortal hand or eye
Dare . . .

A child too embodies them, the fearful
symmetries she sees, the twin stars
of eyes, for instance, that pierce the darkness
of the human face, that make of us

and the gaze before us yet another
animal, our strands of sight knotted
at the pupils, each countenance a cross
between what we can and cannot know.

❧

Once I cranked my window to the night
and saw something of my hand reflected
there, giving off its own warmth, its light.
My view of things chirped on its hinges.

Where there's design, there is a designer,
said the hand, as if the phantom as it
opened the frame were in fact writing
a note, a letter back to the near world.

❧

When William Blake was four, he saw God
put a face to the window and broke out
screaming. Then in time came the angels
that scorched the leaves in the ice of autumn.

In the symmetries of a father's cheeks,
he watched the years carve an effigy,
an homage. In the steady reassurance
of his features, the violence of the new.

The same dull round, that is what you get
when you pray to a clock with one hand,
one motion to wind it, one eyelike gear
that drives the machine of matter and mind.

Any machine, broken or not, will tell you,
there is something in the lower orders
of animals and men, of trees no doubt,
forever messed up and surprised by grace.

❦

The molecule cannot quite decide
the path to life, to death for that matter.
It cheers me up. The absence of a plan.
Then one day a language comes to visit,

the glass of form and the milk that lights it.
There is something explosive in a grain
of sand, like the day we were born.
I see that now. There's nothing without nothing.

❦

Somewhere in a small corner of the Age,
a boy sat shadowed in the leaves and wrote,
in the beginning was a blister of light
that ached into the shape of things. No,

he thought, start again. In the beginning
a man crawled out like a drop of blood.
No again. And on it went, late, long
past dark. In the beginning. In the beginning.

TRINITY

Small things have a different logic to them.
Drop an ant from fifty times its height.
It survives. But a man, a mammoth, a bomb . . .
well, quantum particles tell us, size is fate.
So when Robert Oppenheimer gathered
those great minds, each with his specialty,
they chose a boy's schoolhouse in the heart
of an enormous nation, its sons at sea.
Those days were never simple: the squeak of chalk
against the darkness, the dread of failure,
of success, inside each uneasy thought
the dull knowledge that, hell, if not here,
then some other hell, and so they worked
against the clock, the hammer of its hours.

Trinity. That was their goal, their test site
that drew its name from a line by Donne,
who invited God to *batter his heart,*
God who was *three-person'd,* and so one
conscience split into ravishing light.
The way men long to be that *usurpt towne,*
no doubt it frightens them: the blank slate
that reason fills for all the wrong reasons.
What Oppenheimer saw there, God knows.
Perhaps it was the words *knocke, breathe, shine,*
and seek to mende. Perhaps the overthrow
of one god for another, for one who blinds
the doubt, so we might lie against our shadows
and fall, too deep to fathom, too small to find.

THE DESERT FATHERS

And so when he wandered into the sea
of heat, he gave himself to the mercy

of the waves, the thorns of the dry field,
the clay, the desert bees, the ache that peeled

the tiny twisted flowers drenched in sun,
the water that he walked the reflection

of a power too bright to see, a flood
to glut the blackened rivers of his blood.

Daylight floated the raft of his body
into the hard comfort there, the watery

blur of his vision failing, his sleep short,
diet poor, and he thought of the desert

fathers who came this far for God, they said,
'til the open eye began to dream, to dread

the crush of sky turned bitter as regret.
And so he cast into the distance a net

of prayer which, as such, cannot fathom
the tides that cast their answer into him.

At night, beneath the stars, his eyes pulsed,
the scattered seeds of a universe

lit to liquefy the earth, to ignite
the ground and the raft that sank against it.

He became a speck in the larger mind,
in the drowned face that surfaced with the wind.

This is how it feels, he thought, to be
the orphan of what you sacrifice to see.

And then it came, the surge, the fist that broke
some final lash in an enormous panic,

a terrible crash inside the head he held,
cradled in waves, as if it were a child.

VISITATIONS

1.
Blink

In each eye a little darkness falls.
It snips the cord of light so quick to mend
you hardly see it mending, if at all,

hardly blur beneath the waterfall
of missing things, faster than the mind.
In each eye a little darkness falls

to wet the living glass you cannot feel
against the lid, against the shadow moon
you hardly see. It mends you after all.

You do not think to wipe clean the awful
dust of seeing, the tired world it summons
in. Each eye, a little darkness, falls

asleep, filled though ever unfulfilled,
the way it flutters with what light remains.
You hardly see it mending if, in all

your grief, the blackest of the water spills
its absolution on the day. Amen.
In each eye a little darkness falls.
You hardly see it ending, if at all.

2.

The Missing Link

As a child I looked to the evolution
of things as if it were seamless, this trail
out of the sea, the mud, the fury, the one

bloodline of fish to apes, to early man,
those generations who raised their heads a little
like a child. I looked to the evolution

as a beast parade that would never turn
back, that followed each diminishing tail
out of the sea, the mud, the fury. The one

exhausted mantra on the lips of oceans,
it washed away the shore, the crumbling castle
in each child I looked to. The evolution

of prayer led me ever more uncertain
toward a stumble of dice inside each cell.
Out of the sea, the mud, the fury, the one

god rose each day in the face of the sun,
breaking into many, into animals
as a child I looked to, the free volition
of the sea, the mud, the fury, the one.

3.

Water Clock

The water clock makes into a measure
a flow so continuous none can say
this thing inside the river has a river's

sense of time. The moment of the pour
knows no wheel, no ratchet, no rise of trays
the water clock makes into a measure

we live our lives inside and by. Sure,
there are times the pans that fall are days
we bring inside the river. Is a river's

share of sunlight any less the water
for standing still, any less the race
the water clock makes into a measure.

This body, is it what I am or better,
what I have. So little time to chase
the things inside the river with a river's

speed and thrash. As if leaving were
the comfort we have left, our meeting place
the water clock makes into a measure.
All things in the river become the river.

4.

Hymn

A child sees inside the stained-glass window
the pride of the garden that came before
the hand that raised this smoke, this corpse, this rose.

His mother signals him to pray with those
who come to kneel beneath the candle fire.
The child sees inside their stained-glass window

the petals of the wound that cannot close,
the eye that watches from the atmosphere
the hands that raise this smoke. This force that grows

against the lighted surface here below
presses through his forehead like a fever.
The child sees inside the stained-glass window

a passage from the boredom, the gore, the clothes
that pinch, the goaty voice inside the rafters,
the hands of praise. This smoke, this corpse, this rose,

what are they to him now. What does he know
of a mother's doubt, her ecstasy, her fear.
What child sees inside the stained-glass window
the man that gave this smoke this corpse, and rose.

TALLOW

In de La Tour's *St. Joseph*, the carpenter
leans over the awl in his hands, his sandal
braced against the block, against the stair
that leads us up the cross of the handle,

up these arms exposed to fully realize
the strength in them, up the tourniquet
of his sleeve to the mountainous horizon
of his shoulders, his head, his silhouette

bowed with power. His body stoops to harbor
the meager candlelight his child holds,
the red translucence of the child's fingers
no less a shelter, their wild flame withheld

from us, though we see it in the father's
eye, the way he looks not at his own grip
but at the boy's, the danger there, the fire
that smokes above the glowing fingertips.

Always the missing thing to pull the old
gaze away, however slightly, displaced
by fear that bathes a child's skin in gold,
all things the orphan of some other place.

Even the candle began inside the shadow
of some barn, in the meat of the beast
that gave its life to those here, its tallow
to their room, their labor, the air they breathe.

As for the man who dipped his paintbrush
in the thickening shade—how little we know
of the nights he spent, the weary stretch
of cloth he draped across the morning window.

That he was the son of a baker, sure.
That, as he aged, his canvases took on
the bread and earth tones of what was near,
what lit the quiet of his meditation.

Whatever the history, the painting falls
silent, and so bestows the living space
to move, bemused, free, the way the awl
moves freely inside the mark it makes.
Close your eyes and you see what stains
the air against the back of the craftsman
as if he carries there his own gravestone
where the dates lie down, where they remain.

A chiaroscuro sleepiness encroaches
on the boy, the cloistered universe
made of blood and oil, of red that reaches
through the char to warm the midnight in us.

In each pupil a bead of black wax
as if sight began in dark, to better bind
man to child, the fire to its wick,
the blush of tallow to the living hand.

THE RAISING OF THE BELLS

Not only were the largest of the church bells cast
in pits, there, beneath the thrusting of the tower,
at times the earthly founding of a bell came first,
when walls rose above the mold, above the flower

of bronze they sexed with a clapper, then block-and-tackled
from the ground into some hymn or other, some knell
invoking praise or mourning, or both, the *chain-toll*
for instance, moving from the smallest of the bells

to the gravity of the huge—a descent of sorts
and yet the iconography of yearning upward,
of growing old toward the striking of the notes
all at once, a kind of last breath, a final word.

Or better yet beyond all words, the muscle and peal
that threshes the blue with dire hope. It longs to reap
as it sows, to lay spring's harvest at our table.
All at once. What sound could be more complete

and yet discordant, unresolved. It knocks the sky
in joy, in anger, as if it were a child that throws
its toy. All at once. And then the long decay
like smoke, the plea that rises as the silence grows.

AIR

Long ago my house went up
in flames, and as I held my robe
closed, standing in the street,
I was too young to miss my things.
That is what I told myself.
My mother wept the dry tears
of disbelief, her face a terror
beneath the angel on its cross.
After all a house on fire's
a thing of glory, a monster.
And yes, I shuddered. I thought
I was cold. And then, I was.

All my life I have stared
at fire as if it were the bridge
between no thing and all things.
A kind of language that way,
the glass of snakes in the river,
a mirror that pours into a mirror.
I buried a lot of losses there
talking to no one. Who hasn't.
To feel the warmth of paper
as the words darken and writhe.
The opposite of nothing is not
everything. It is one thing.

Once I got so ill, so miserable,
I died a little, and my season
dismantling the emptiness taught me
I am always there, in the music
of thought that blooms out of nowhere
and so returns. Space was full

in the way that objects were not.
Mad, I know, but it made a better song,
more comfortable with silence.
One synapse darkened its lantern
and looked out at the house of stars
that fell to pieces like a monster.

When I first learned the notes
in my hands, my father listened,
hearing in the strings a meadow.
Entire heads of tunes returned
like a phone call or beautiful soldier.
Or the carriage of a typewriter
as it drafts its final testament.
Every song was, for me, a phantom
armature to hang my nerves on.
The arcs of pitches falling back
to earth, they became the bones
in the body that nothing never had.

Spirit, like fire, longs for something
to move and space to move it.
Just this morning a man exploded
his body for God, and I saw
in pictures of the blaze something
of the nothingness he died to fill.
But what do you say to silence
in its own tongue. Bless us
children of no particular word,
we who bear our wounded through
the strain of vaulted ceilings, a crosshair
above us that blossoms into smoke.

❖ IV ❖

FOR THE LOST CATHEDRAL

1.

One life, one life, one life, and so
the secret life, it began so shyly,
glittering the highest branches,

breaking in droplets over the rooftops,
a near mist, he thought, so quietly it came.
And though it seemed to fall

over everything, every gesture and scrap
of clothing, every word escaping
his lips, though it lengthened

its low green blades in the morning sun,
it lay forever at a distance
like the crackle of a river

becoming always something else,
the missing thing that bears the name
of the river. That bears the voice:

To split your life into two lives, yours
and the secret's, to divide the mind,
to break your death into two deaths now,

as if to multiply that one last breath
so that it might shatter into two breaths,
and four, a whole flock of breaths,

to bury yourself in the living choir.

2.

There are men, he thought, who grip
the secret so hard it shrinks
to the size of a fist, incarnate,

men who light his TV at dusk,
who lay their lives at the footstool
of the secret, unable to look up,

fierce with the shame that is their goodness.
Iconography flutters on a wall
like the papered shrine of a stalker's closet.

There are men who envy
the sweethearts of martyrs,
men whose death is the bride

of the secret, who slip into a ring
of wire, ribbed in explosives,
who cry out the way a lover cries,

in abandonment, in prayer.

3.

Though no one knows the truth
of the secret's birth, no one
would presume it had one

as we know it, there are tales—
like the story of the woman
downed in the booby-trapped jungle,

far from home, seeing
in her broken skin the arrival
of a force, the sheer gore

a glory, which, if not the secret,
is nevertheless its messenger,
the speed of the angel

come in a flash to fill that gap.
God, she said, cursing, *God,* again
more softly now, like a call

to no one no one intended,
not fully, just the rising
apparition on her lips, a language

pouring from the open wound.

4.

What's a name, he asked,
that some would give it freely
to each thing they love save

the whole of love, this thing
that is nothing and all of it,
this wish that moves from near

to far, the very wits of near,
the very far that loves to surpass
the far. What's in a voice

as if names were ours and so the named.
Look at the names of the field
where the weather wears them.

You see a girl with a finger
in the grooves of letters.
As if names were flesh and so the named.

To put the secret anywhere
he thought less of words
than of the eye, the circled circle,

how named or nameless we enter
at a distance. Just like a circle
to love a distance, to be

both womb and portal, rose
and world, the hold of the well
and the round voice of empty space:

is there anyone there, there, there.

5.

And so we arrive: here
at the house of the secret,
beneath the vaulted

stars of the sanctuary
dome, our voices made tall
by ceilings that gasped,

walls that coiled at the rim
like giant scrolls of water
inhaled out of the seas.

Such was the rapture
he conjured, having washed
at such an altar, its glass rose

a single mighty eye ahead.
Unthinkable, he thought,
the heft of caution in this,

our hospice. Irresistible,
the quiet in the shudder
of the psalm and prelude.

Go. Sleep.
Bewilder what you calm.
The sound of rain goes

where the rain cannot.

6.

His instinct of the holy was never
the chosen and so not holy enough.
His instinct of the more holy

was how he walked gently like a fly
on a pool of fresh rain. His instinct
of the secret was how childhood saw

the great unflinching eye that notes
all things, the name that would hold fast
the river, the river that holds the gaze

of names. Which is to say he needed
a greater vantage point than any
man or name. He needed a Lord

the way a body needs a brain,
the way some of us need to see the King
as what he rules. Long live the King.

A child rules a world of toys.
She does not know where she ends,
the toys begin. Of those who watch,

who, if any, she will survive.

7.

For those who made the journey,
a relic held the forever fading
breath of the secret, not the body

entire but the broken parts
that would one day be a body
in kind: the tooth of our Lord,

a psalm of hair, the foreskin
that brought a saint to tears,
the many foreskins of, praise God,

a single saint—each sacrament more
radiant beneath the touch.
He understood that touch,

the sacrifice that blazed
the paths of pilgrims,
the unforgiving paths that bent

their backs. Not to lose
the secrecy, but to give it
the ghost of some possession,

to give our own flesh that ghost,
that gift of the passage
from the near to the far,

to the nearness of the far.
But that was long ago. The paradise
of relics is a relic now.

Some were lost among the catacombs.
Others burned as fakes.
As if a secret died

in each, or if not died
then burned a bit, knelt down
at the shadow of the shroud

and ate.

8.

But what about the flood.
Pestilence, answers the world,
a baptism of disease.

And so the secret threw
flowers like specks of blood.
There, it said, *what secret would be less*

than its creation.

9.

And then a conflagration spread across
the face of a holy land
which was the cradle of secrets,

entire desert minefields of secrets;
which took the multitudes
for the few, the few for the many;

where the spirit of revenge was rage
against time—take it back:
these words made of sticks and cinders,

of the near at hand, iconography
scratched on prison walls.
Take back the wailing wall of paradise.

The star-spit of the rifle and fuse,
the cavernous bunker thumped
and smoking, brimming with ink—take that.

Take the secret few the sun takes down
like rain, like rust, like a deposition.
Or the sacred ground that opens

its mouth and nothing comes.
Gather up the slow fuel of the multitudes
smeared in oil, entire desert

minefields of oil. Wash them,
name them, carry them off.
Bear them up through the story

you hand your children
like a gun, like all the world
dragged through needle of heaven,

and see what you have left.

10.

The night the secret died he was out
walking the woods, their leafy shadows
eclipsing the stars, and the trees

which long had been the legs of the sky
were no longer legs, and the stones
sealed up their boxes of jewels,

and that flinching in the branches,
the first scant sparks of rain descending,
had nothing to do with fire and angels,

being no more, he thought, than *rain*,
though even this as he said it, the word
with its arms full of leaves, waking,

was just another sound among many,
just another wind to wander overhead,
desireless among its kind,

without a place to kneel or suffer.

11.

for Stephen Crane

One life, one life, and so the multitudes
return. A secret dies in each
and so returns.

He considered the courage of living
without the secret,
how, for all he knows,

a secret admires that way of being
friends, of opening the palms
of prayer like a boat

exposed to heavy water.
There are days when heaven falls
silent, when the secrecy

does away with the secret.
Always more flowers
in the field than hands

to hold them. Some lie
on the beds of the multitudes.
They are the rivers of the field

ever losing the thing
that bears their name.
They are the small wind

that waves the fallen colors of the many,
the sun-drenched river
of the near to the far,

the joys of the field above our names
ever becoming something
corruptible, nameless, something

else. Praise them.

CPSIA information can be obtained
at www.ICGtesting.com
Printed in the USA
LVHW032119090323
741291LV00020B/331